Parasports

Contents

Written by Abbie Rushton

Collins

How parasports started

Parasports began in the 1940s.
Parasport events were started to help
men injured in the conflict.

Crowds supported the contestants as they took part in sports. Parasports have transformed across the years, and now there are lots of events and sports.

Parasports are sports for contestants with impairments. You need lots of skill to do parasports at a high level.

Parasports are fair for all contestants. Contestants with similar impairments run, jump or swim to win!

Swimming

This contest is for sight-impaired swimmers. "Tappers" stand at the end of the pool.

tapper

They tap the swimmers to tell them when to turn. Then the swimmers can speed down the pool!

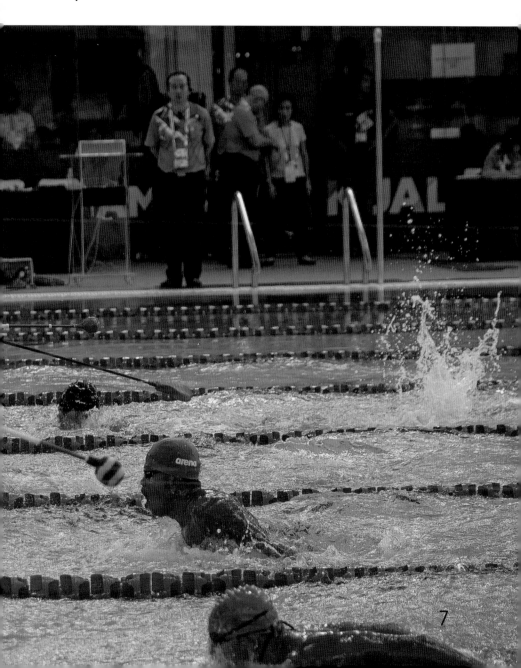

Athletics

Para-athletic sports are events such as:

- flinging a discus, javelin or shot put
- running
- jumping.

Contestants must train hard.

discus

javelin

shot put

WC 415

running

jumping

Powerlifting

This is powerlifting. The powerlifter is flat on a bench.

She has three lifts – down to the chest, then up.
The best lift is recorded.

Smashing records!

This is Markus. He shattered the long-jump record.

This is Kadeena. In 2021, she smashed a record for speed on the track.

Parasports for children today

Children with impairments can do parasports too.

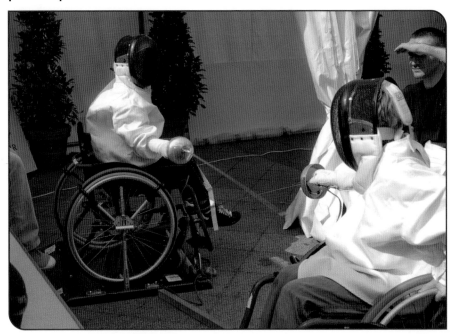

Training helps you keep fit and have fun!

You can join a sports club. You will meet lots of children! You might meet children like you.

Index

Columba

Columba had problems with speech until he was six.

Now, Columba is a fantastic runner. He smashed the 400 m record!

Melissa

Melissa lost a leg in 2004. She is an expert in lots of sports!

Melissa helps children and adults with impairments get into sport.

Parasports

 Review: After reading

Use your assessment from hearing the children read to choose any GPCs, words or tricky words that need additional practice.

Read 1: Decoding

- Encourage the children to practise reading words with adjacent consonants. Remind them to try splitting longer words into chunks if it helps them.

  im/pair/ments   ath/let/ics   swimm/ers   con/test/ants   train/ing

- Point to shorter words with adjacent consonants, such as **smashed**, **speed**, and **track** on page 13. Say: Can you blend in your head when you read these words?

Read 2: Prosody

- Model reading page 12, emphasising **Markus** and **He**. Point out how you used emphasis to connect the name with the pronoun.

- Ask the children to read page 13, reminding them to use emphasis in the same way for clarity. Check they emphasise **Kadeena** and **she**.

Read 3: Comprehension

- Ask the children to describe any parasport stars they already know about. Ask: What is their sport? What have they achieved?

- Ask: How did parasports start? Refer to pages 2 and 3, and discuss why it was a good idea. How might the men have felt before parasports started?

- Turn to pages 22 and 23, and ask the children to choose a photo. Ask them to look back through the book to find information about the sport shown, before feeding back to the group. Remind them they can use information from the photos as well as from the words.

- Bonus content: Ask the children to compare the information on Columba and Melissa on pages 18 to 21. Ask: In what ways are their achievements similar? How do you think they feel about their achievements? Do you find them inspiring? Why?